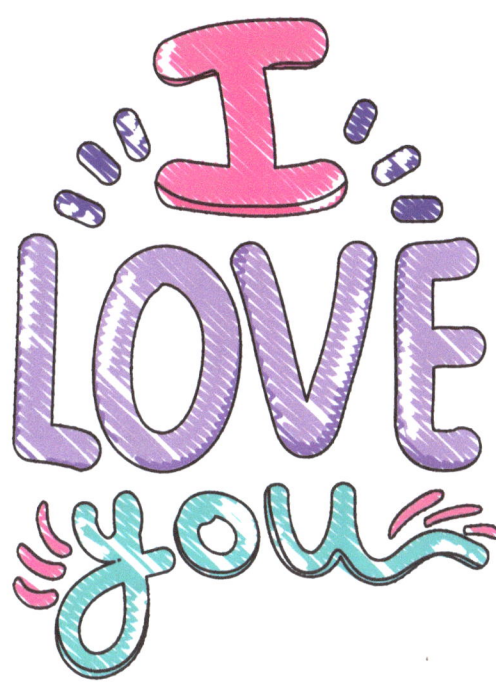

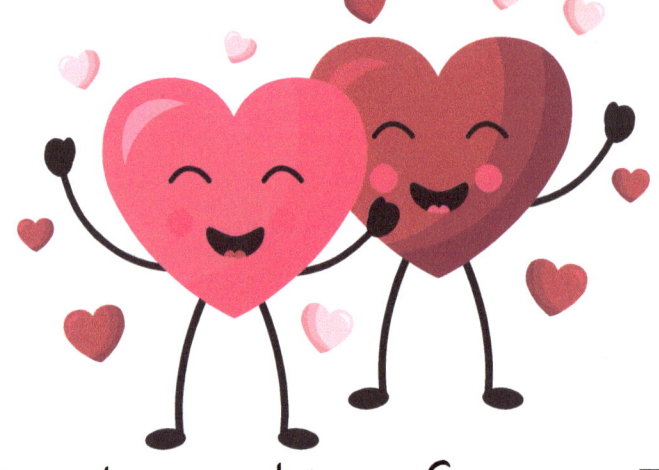

If it's not a problem for you, I would greatly appreciate, If you could leave your feedback in the review section on Amazon once you're finished reading. This means so much to me.

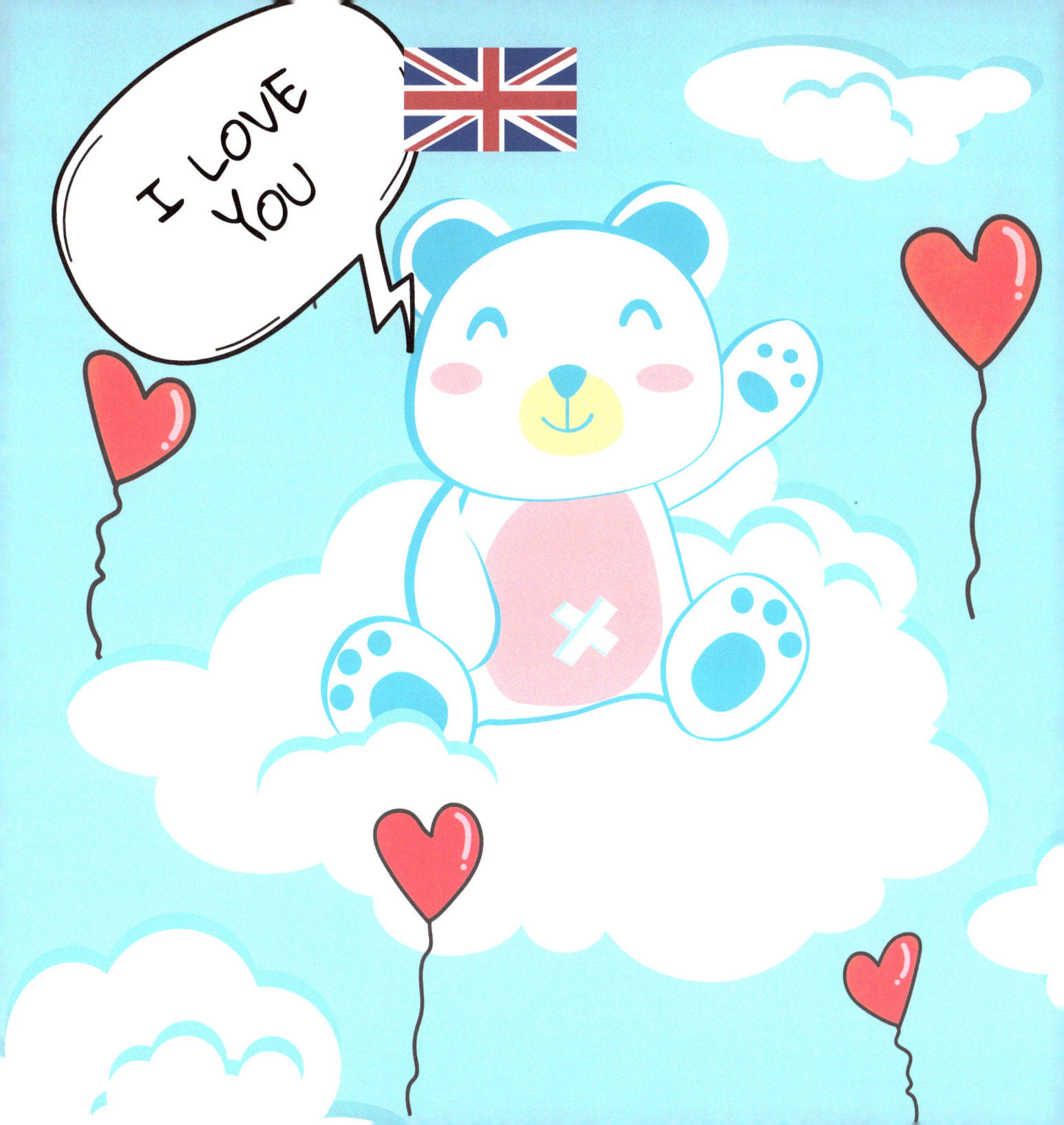

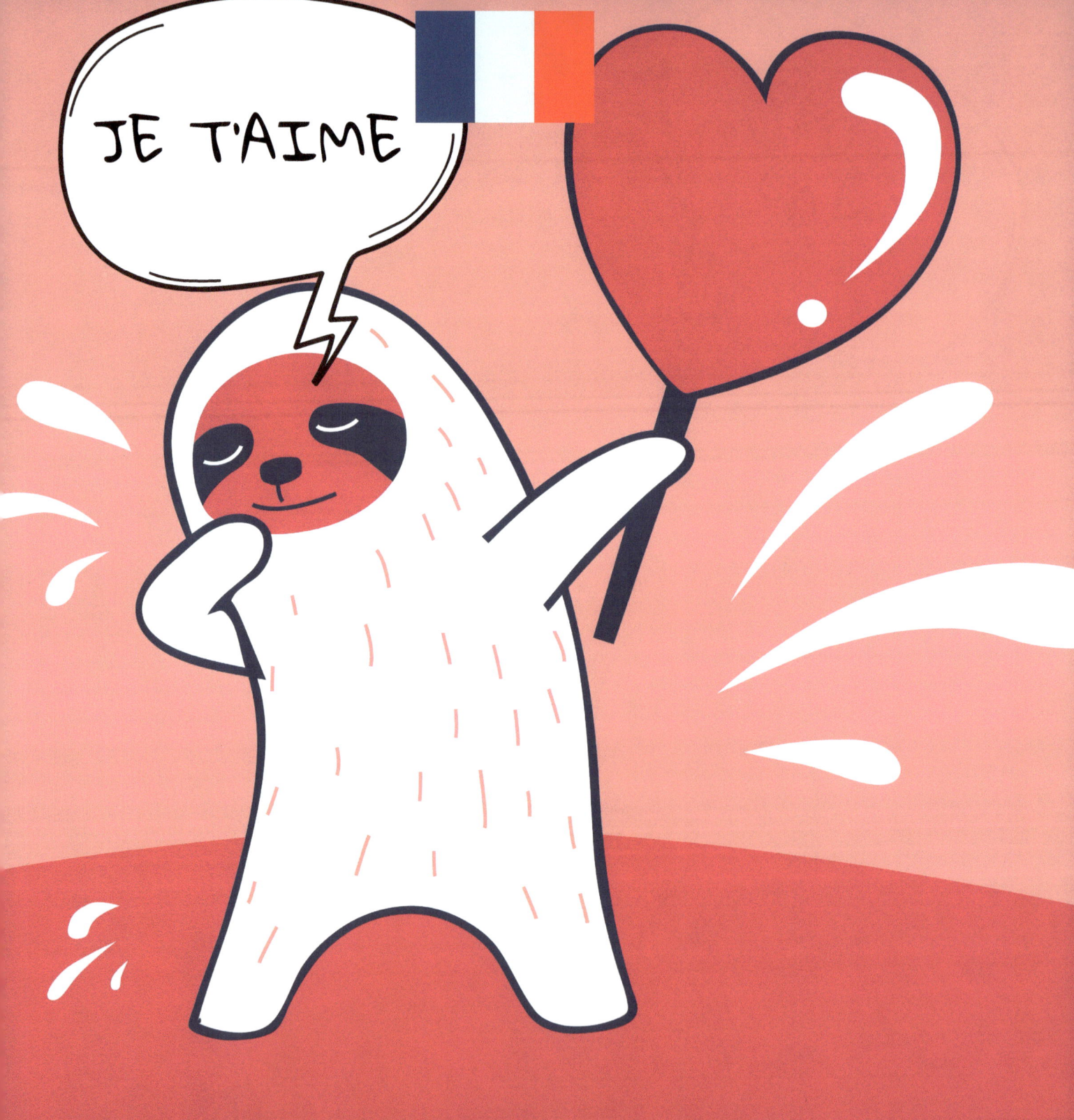

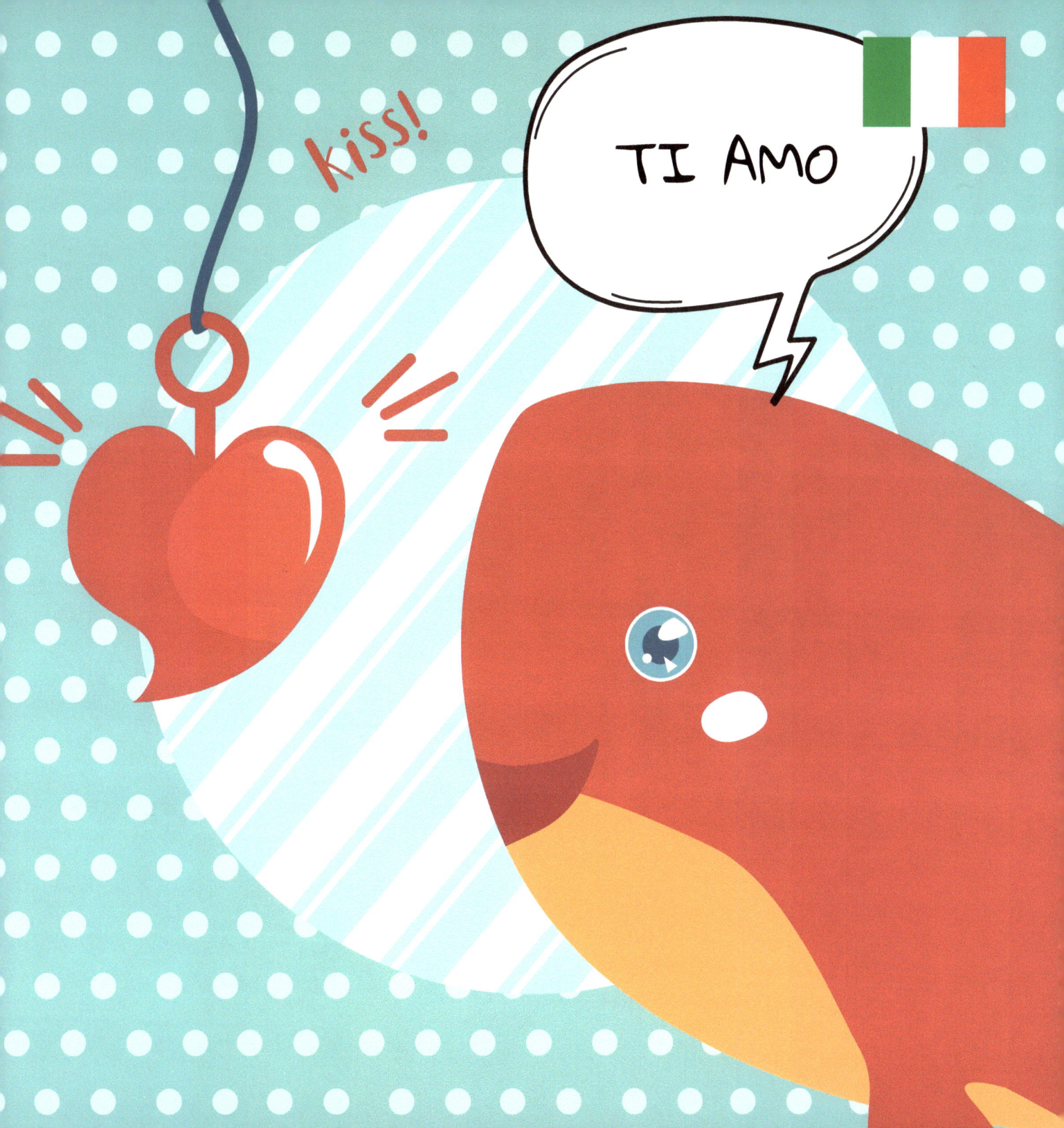

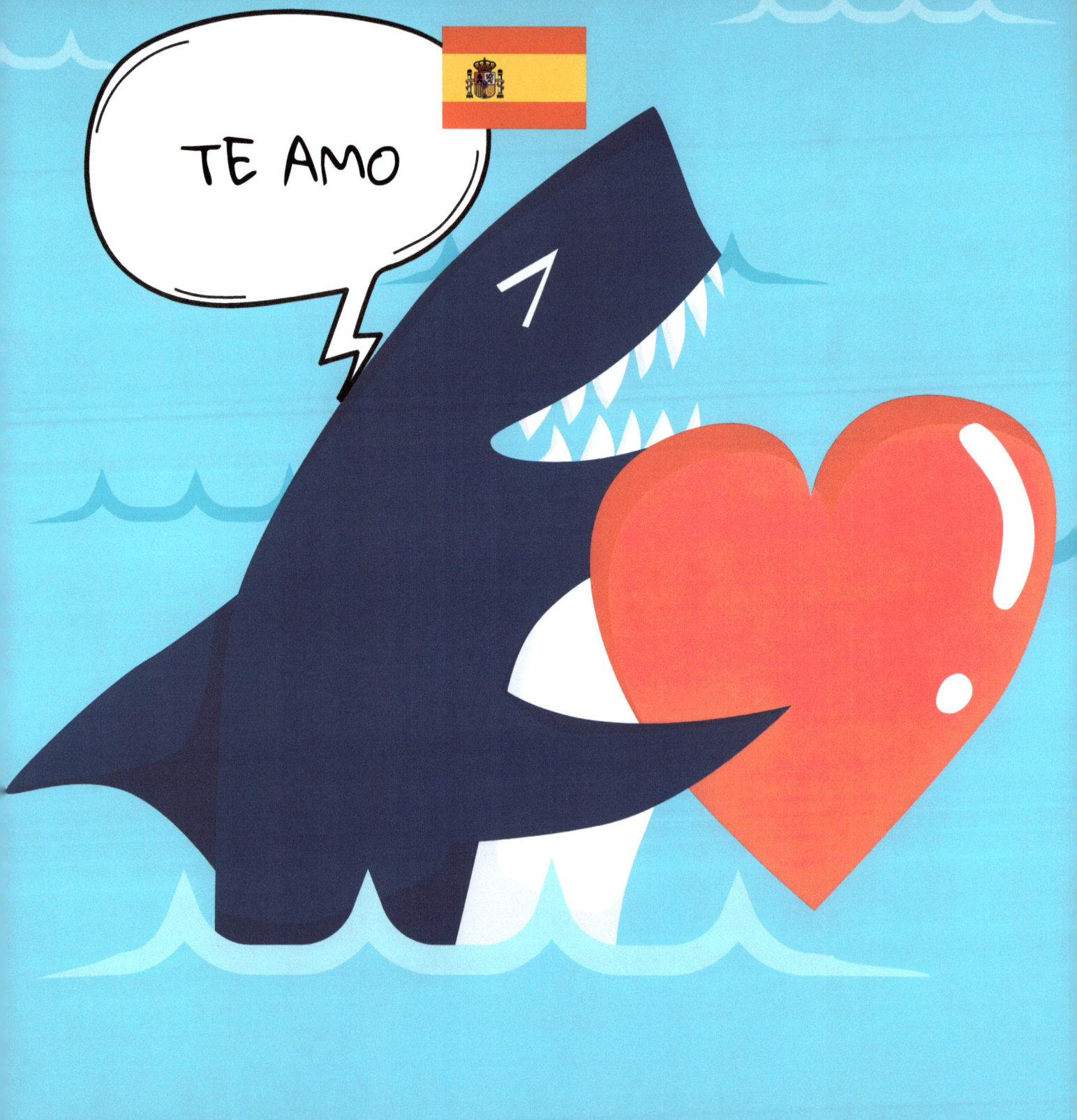

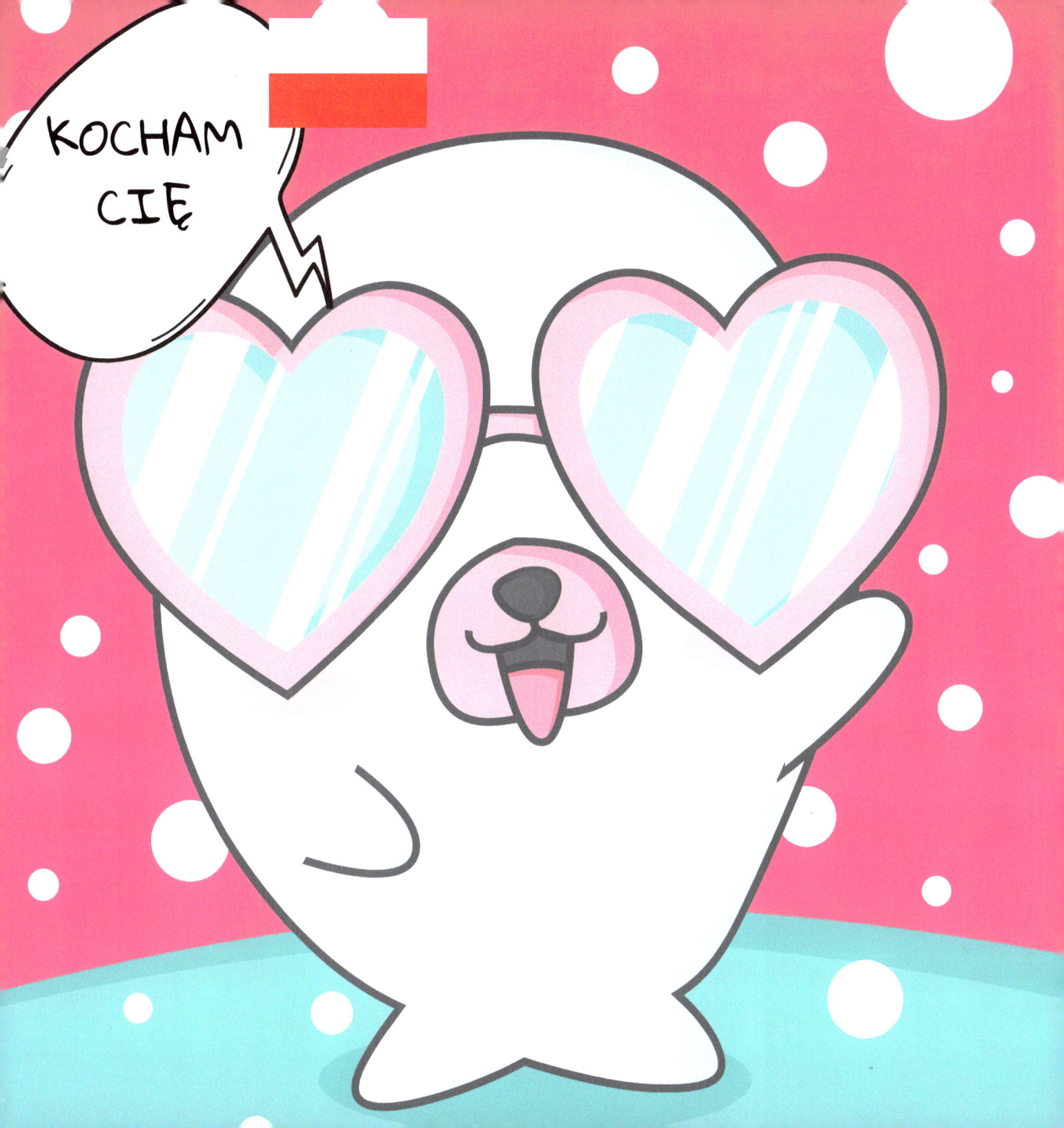

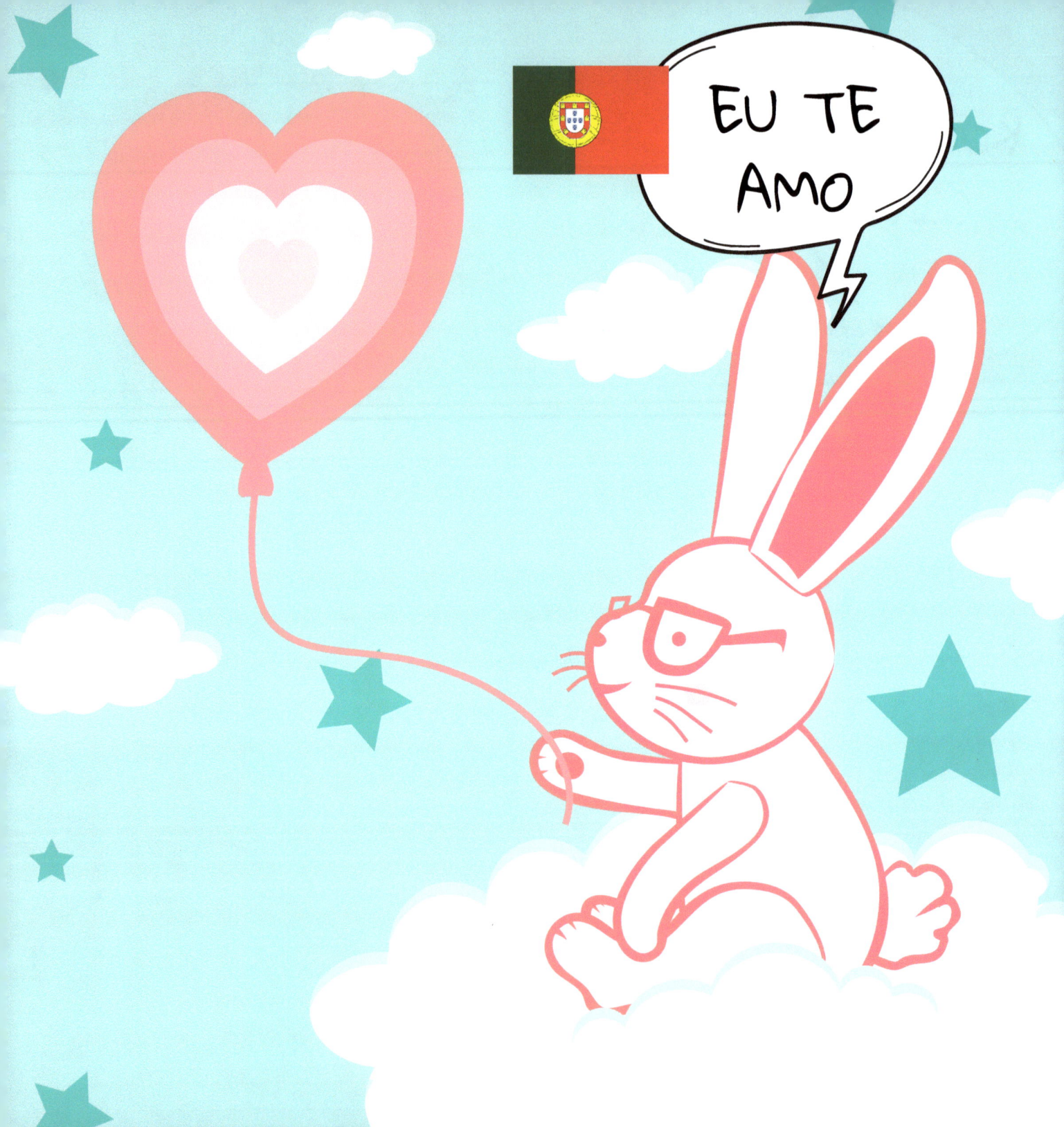

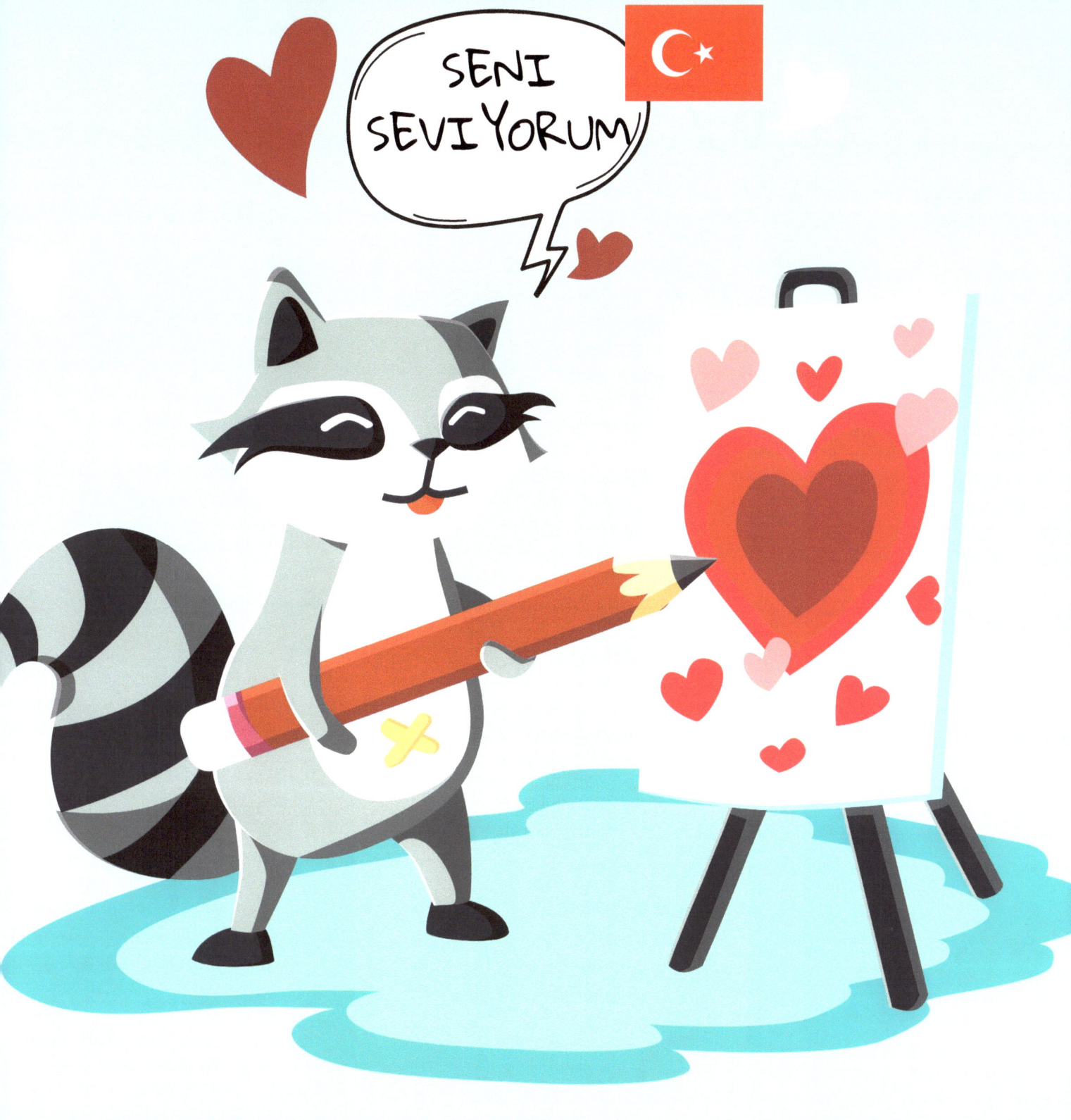

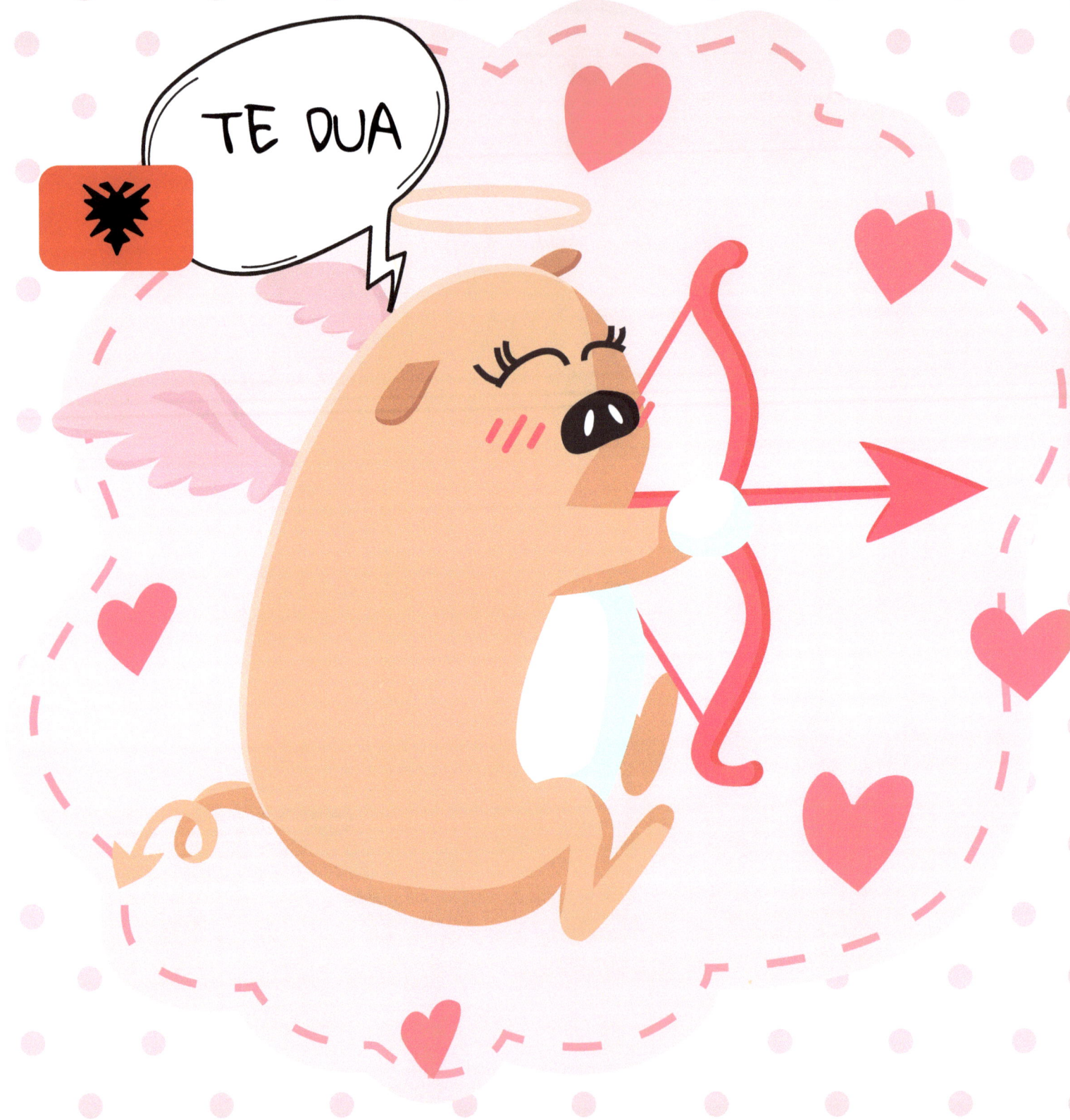

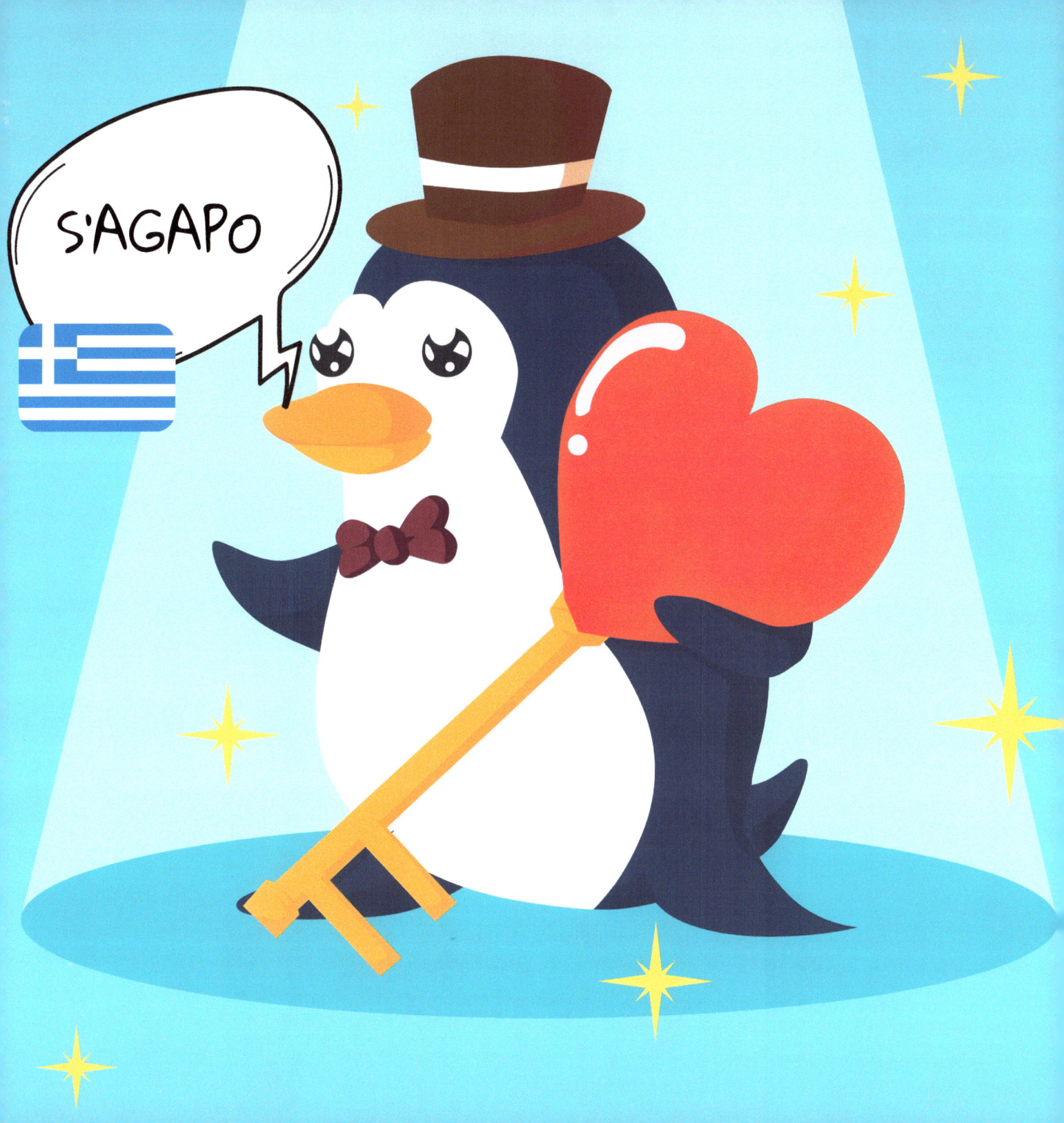

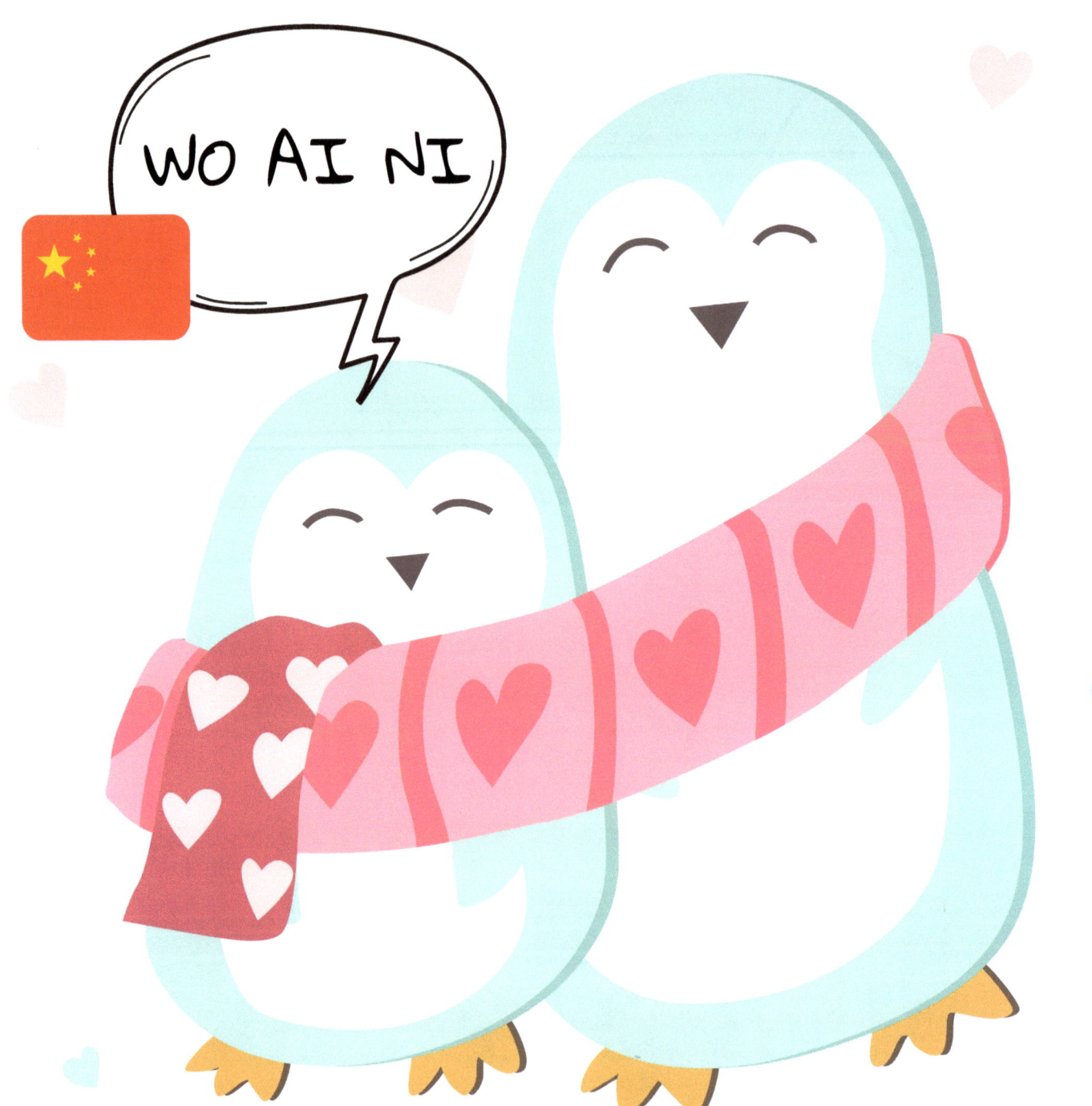

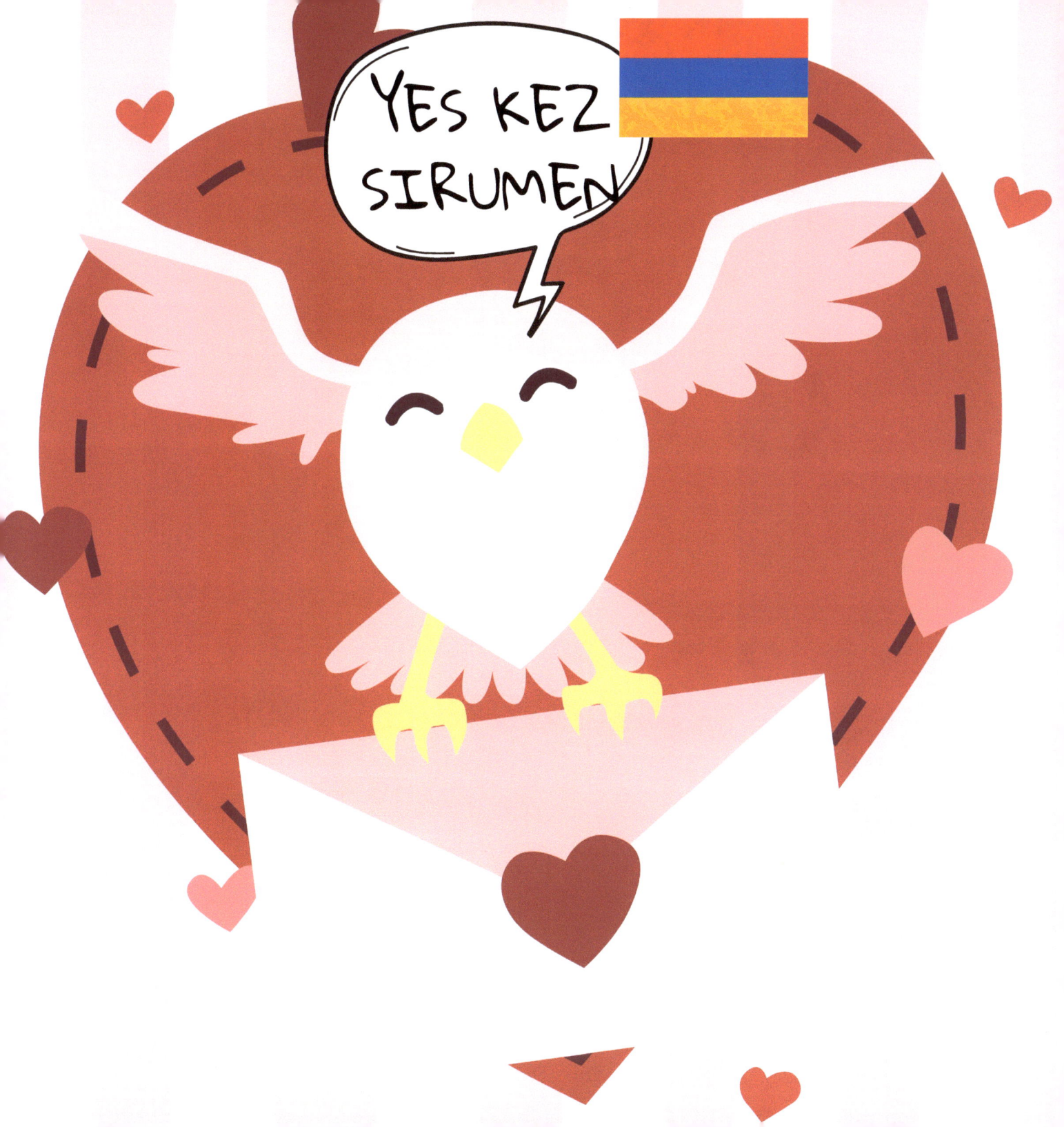

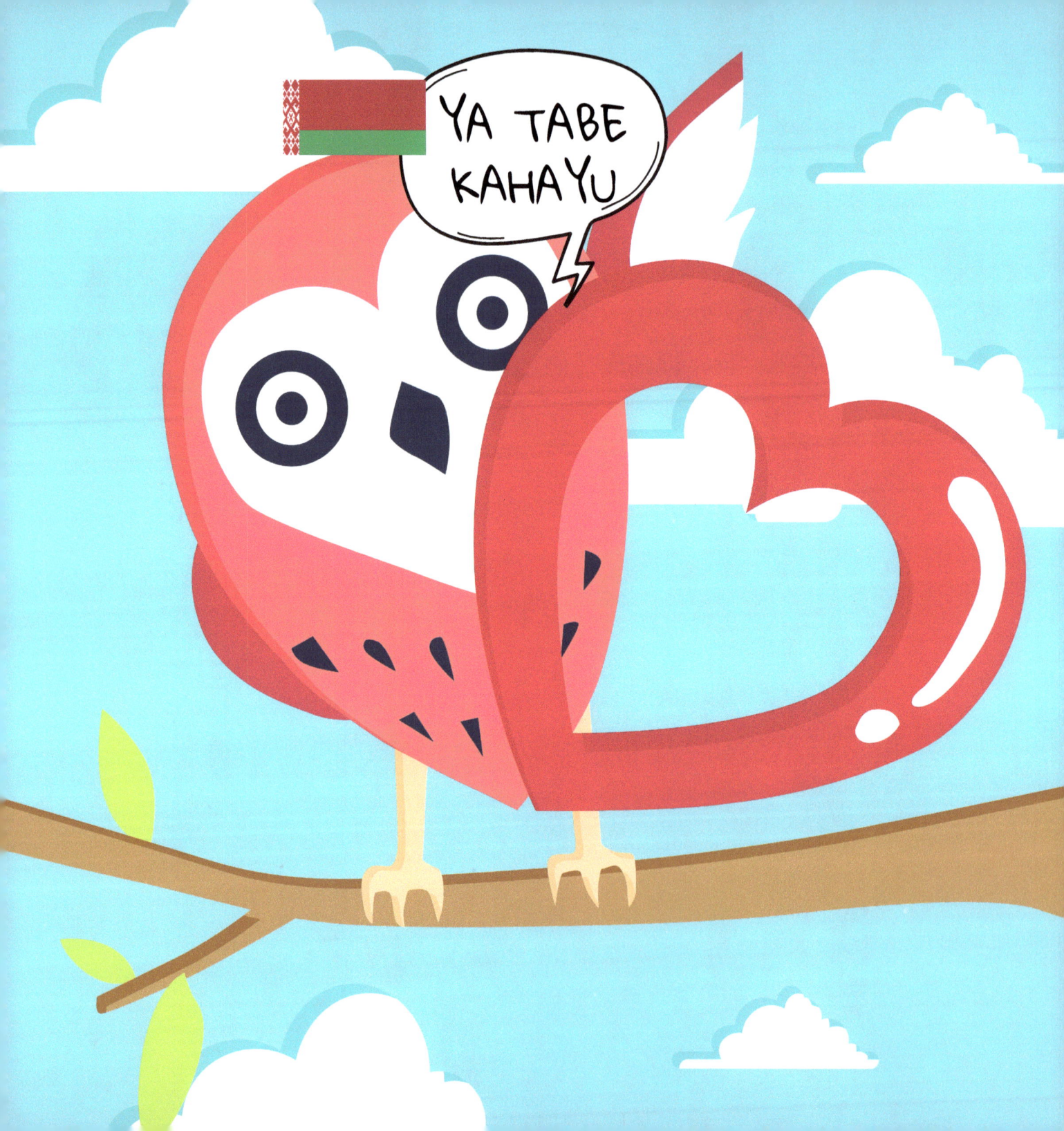

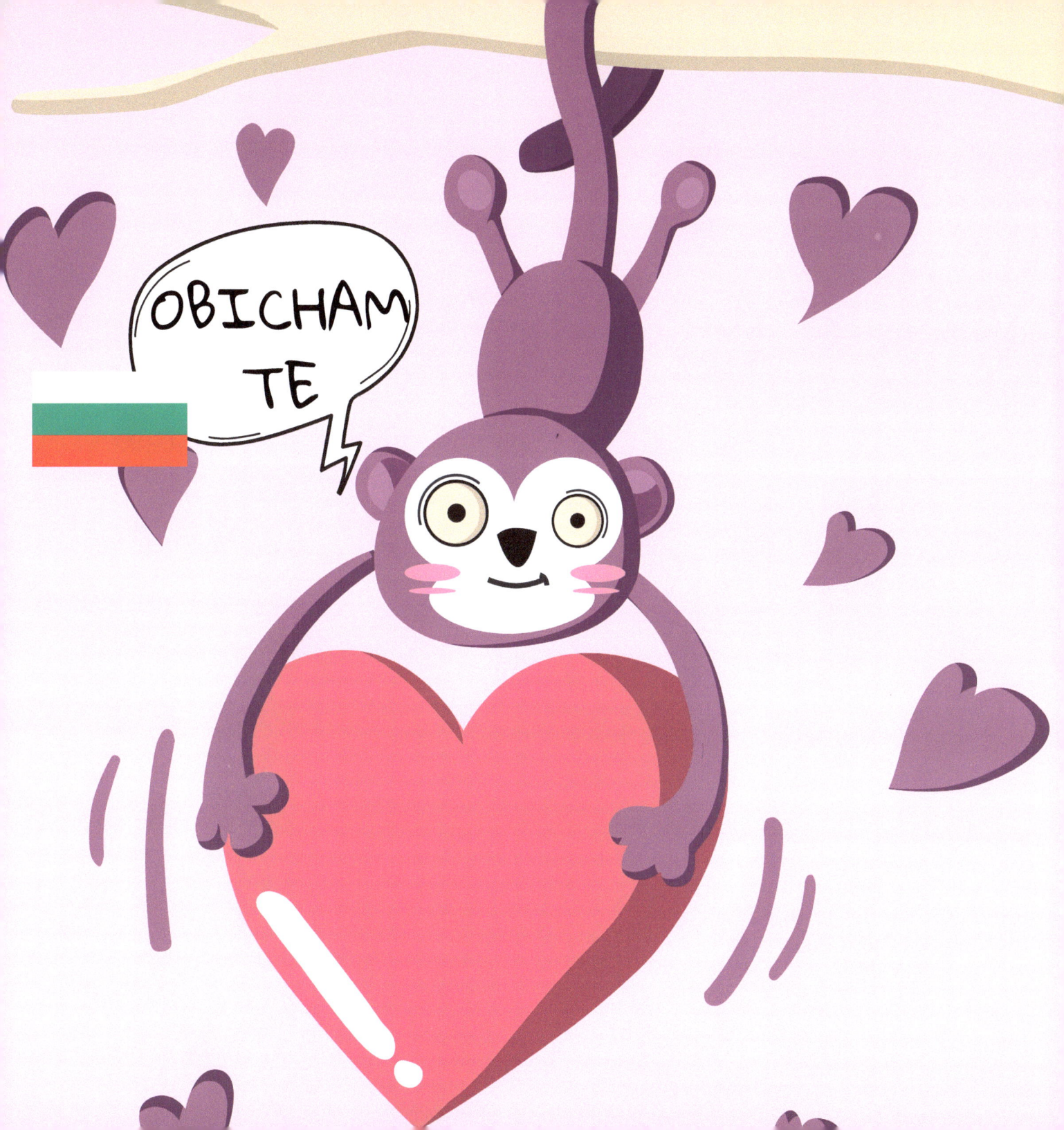

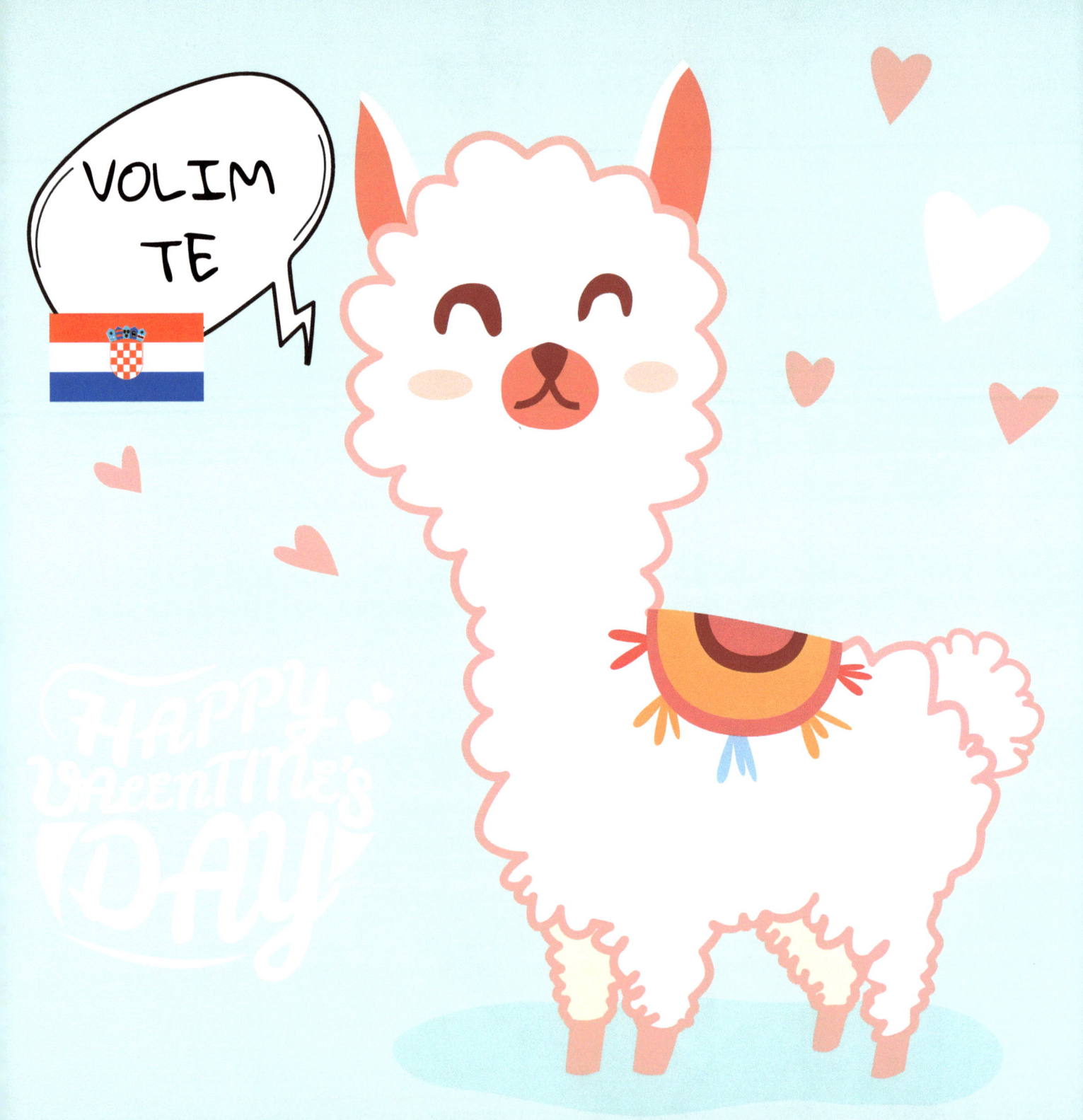

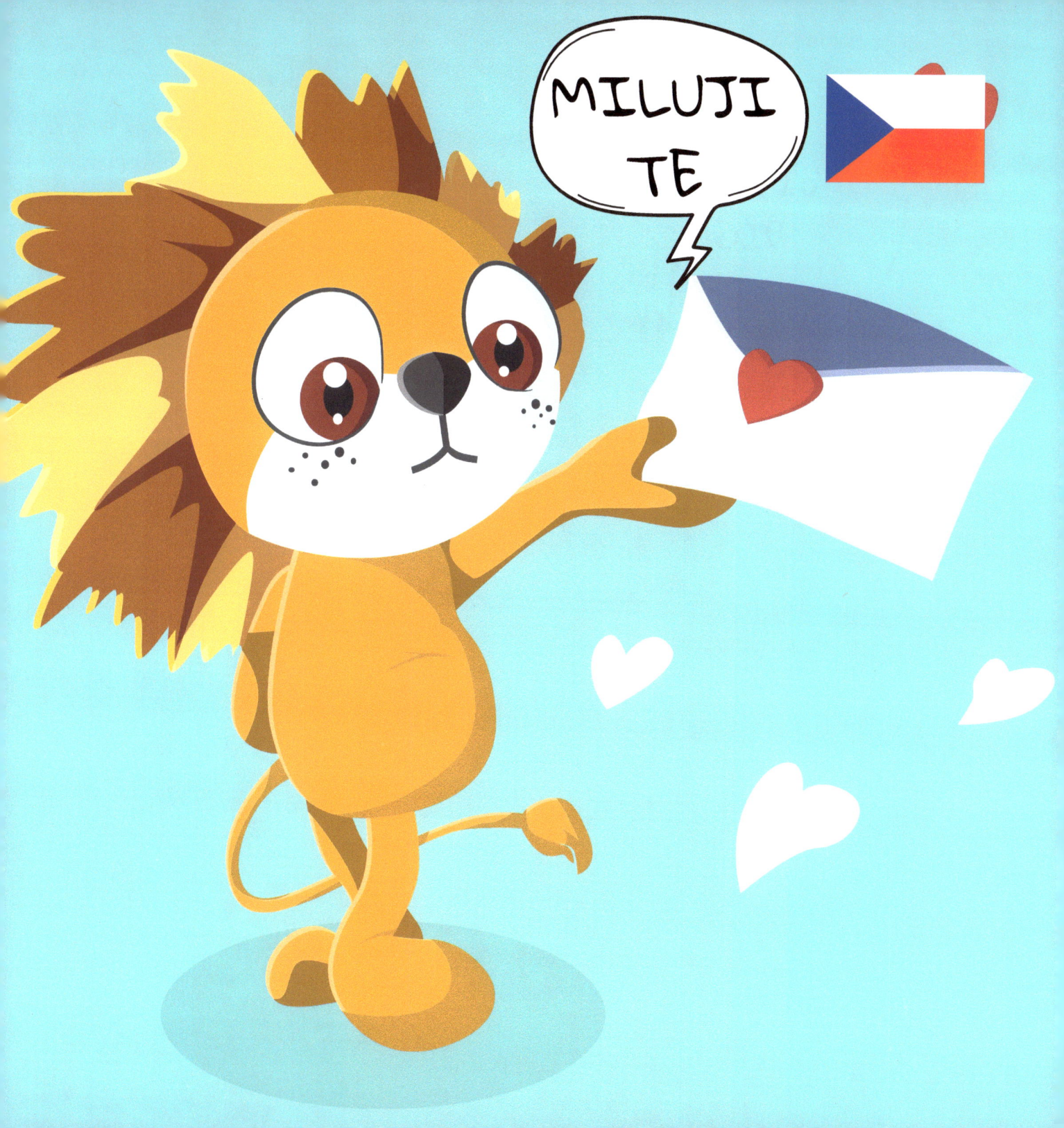

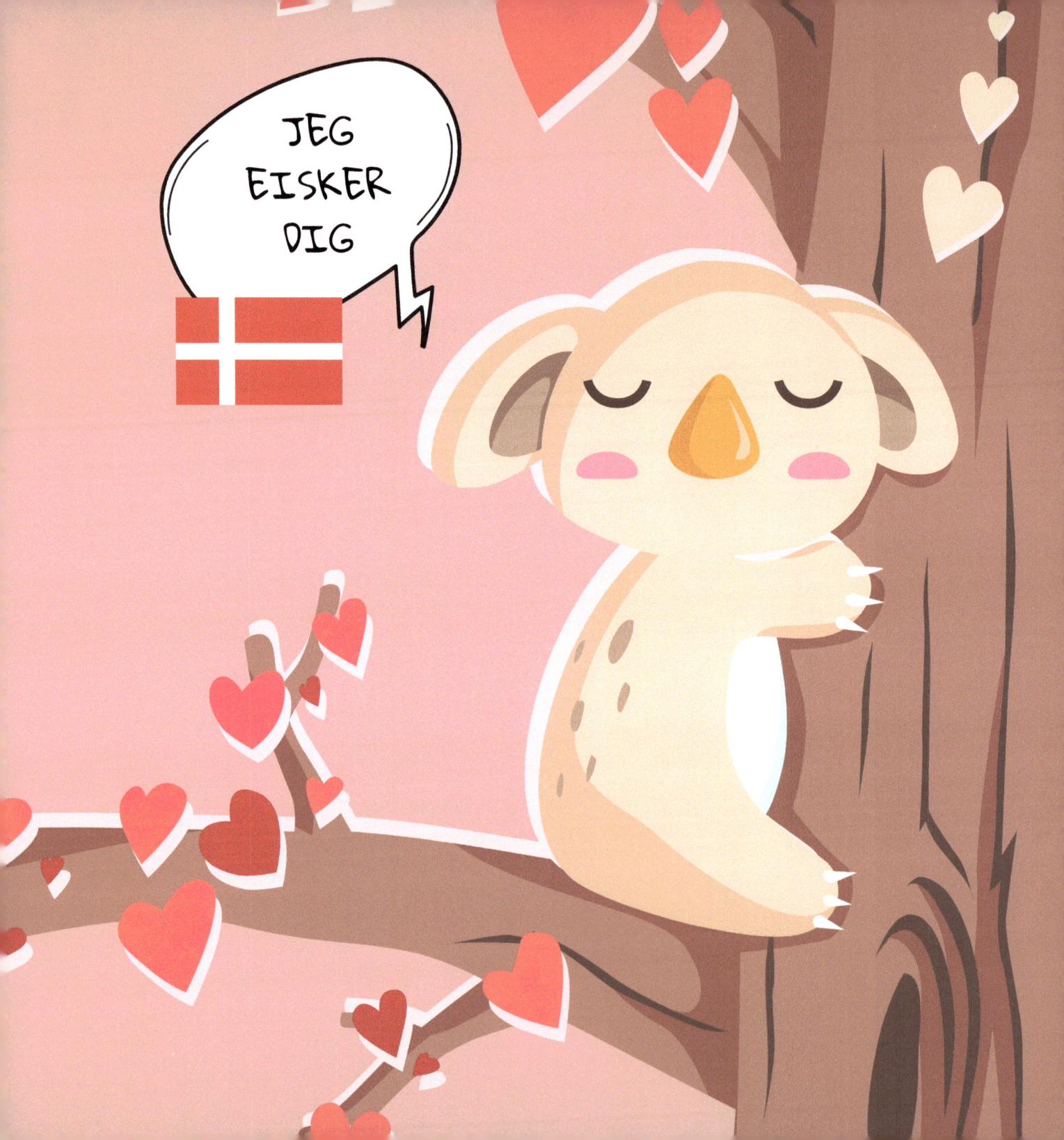

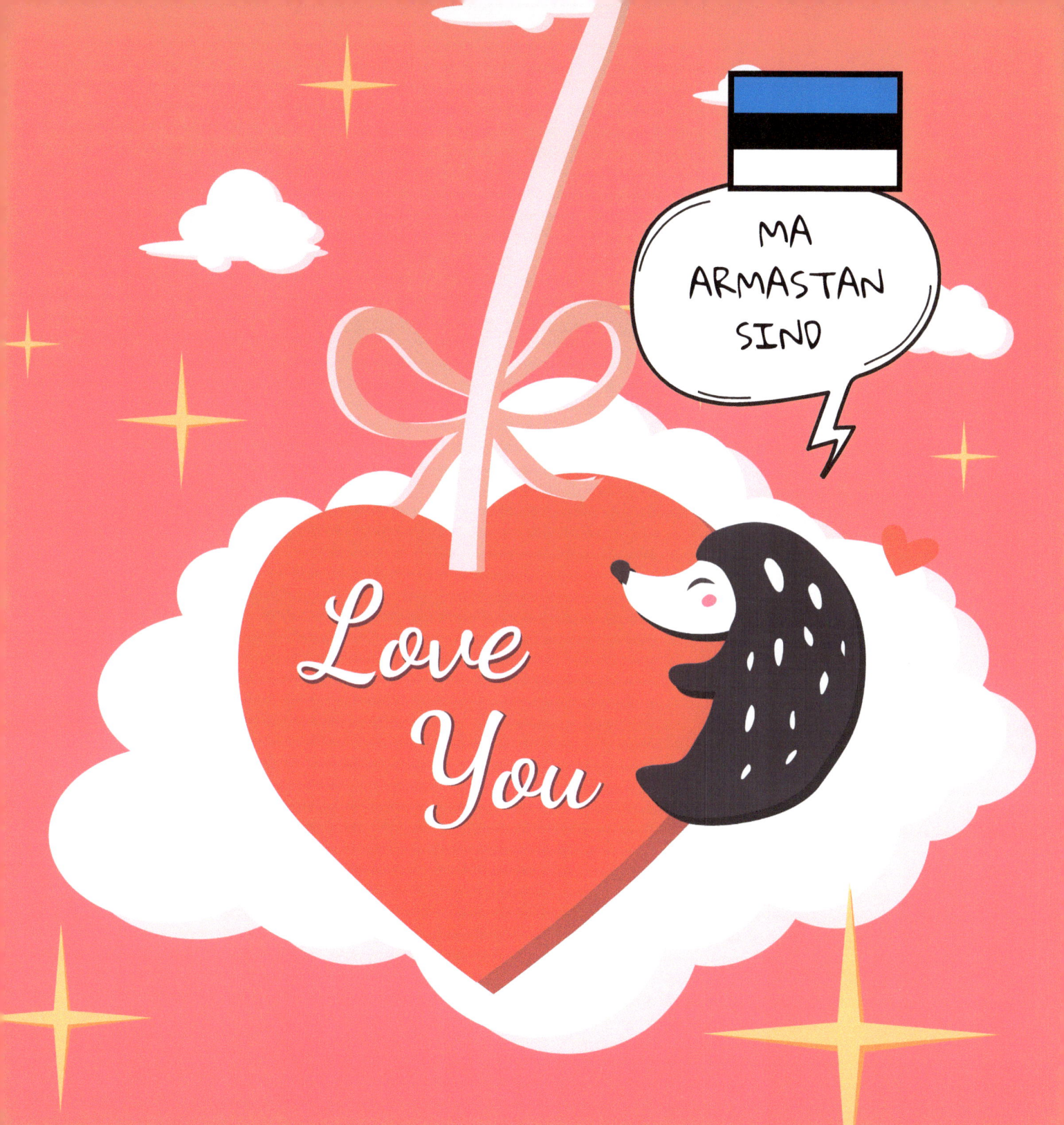

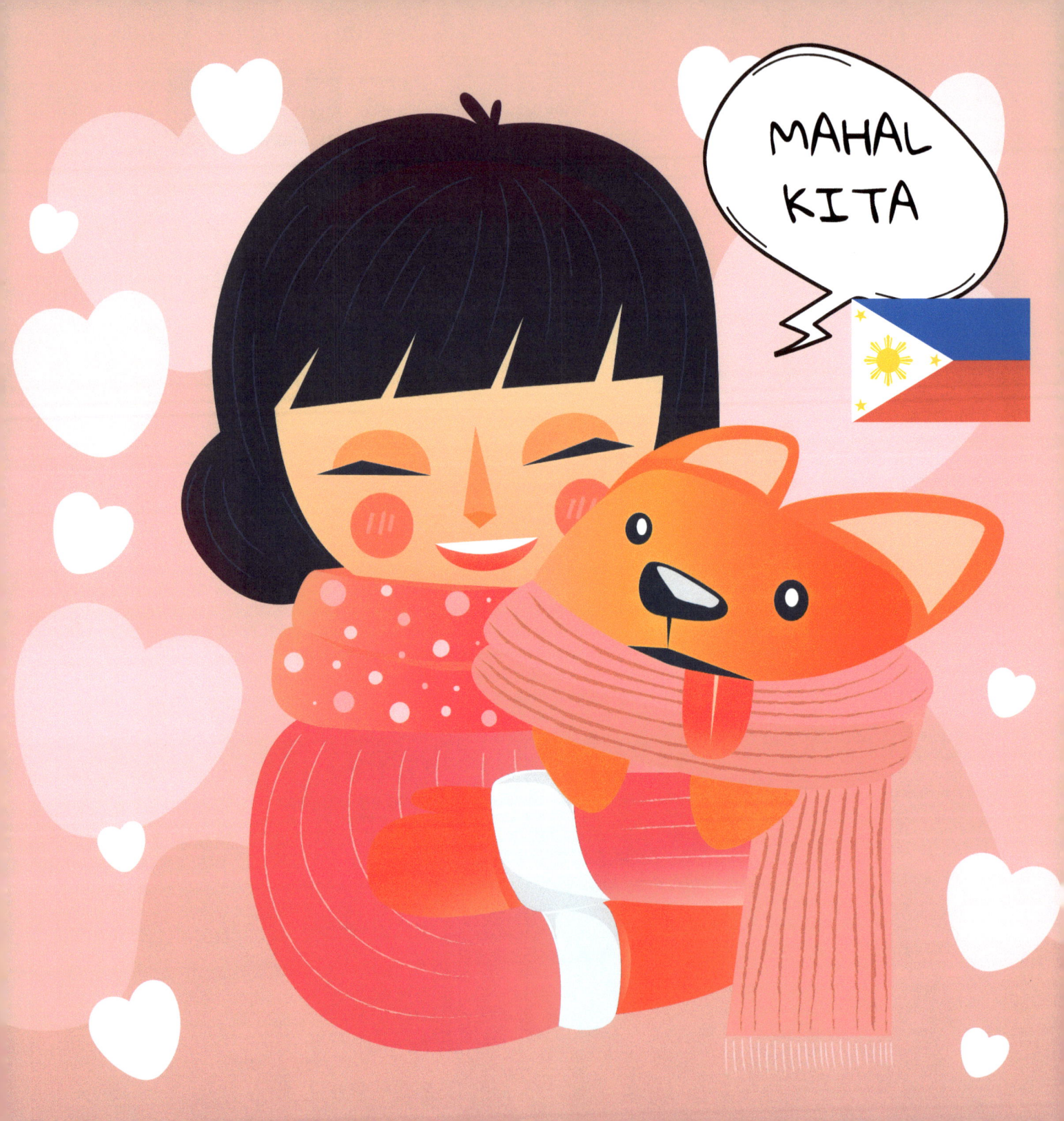

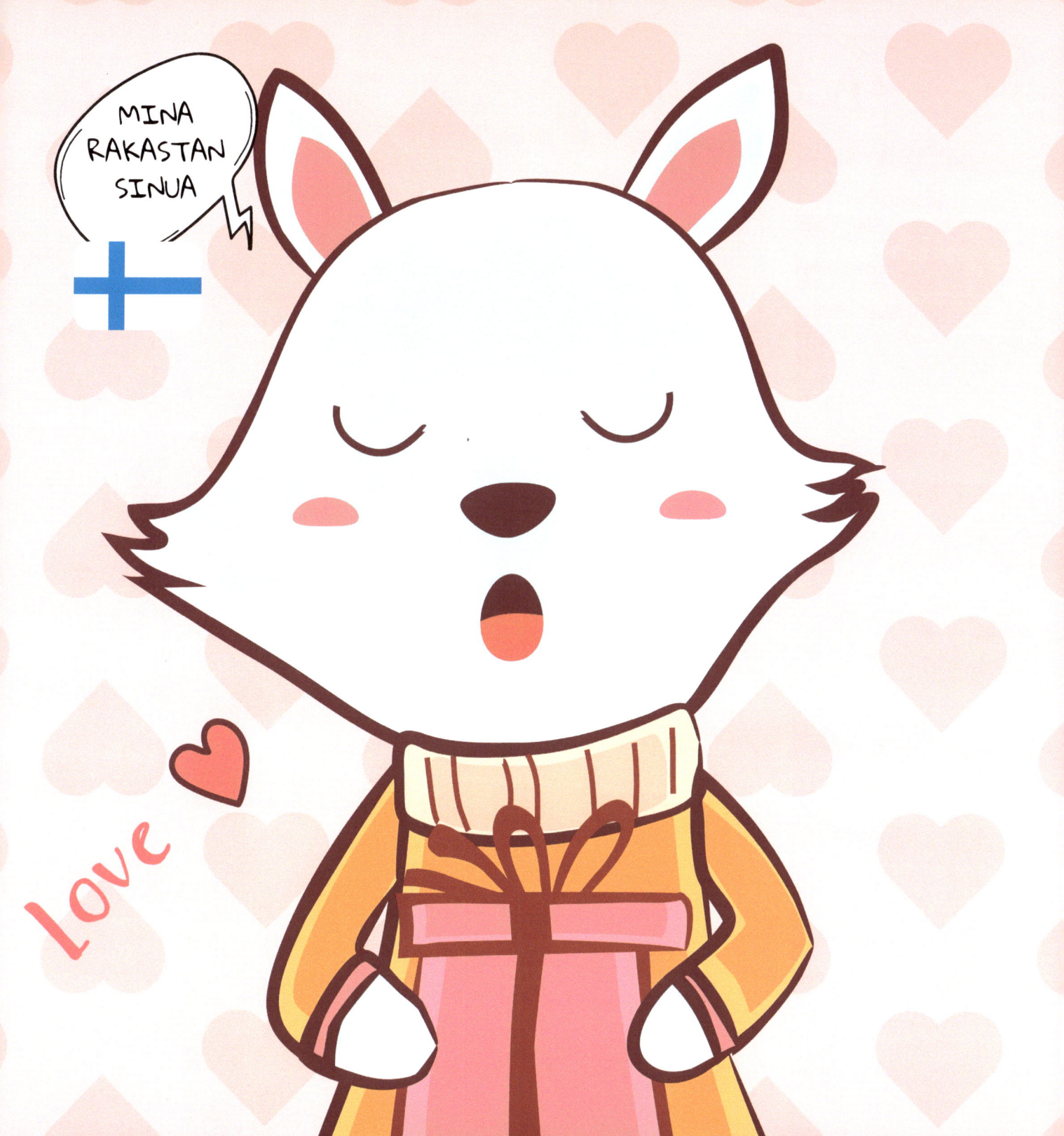

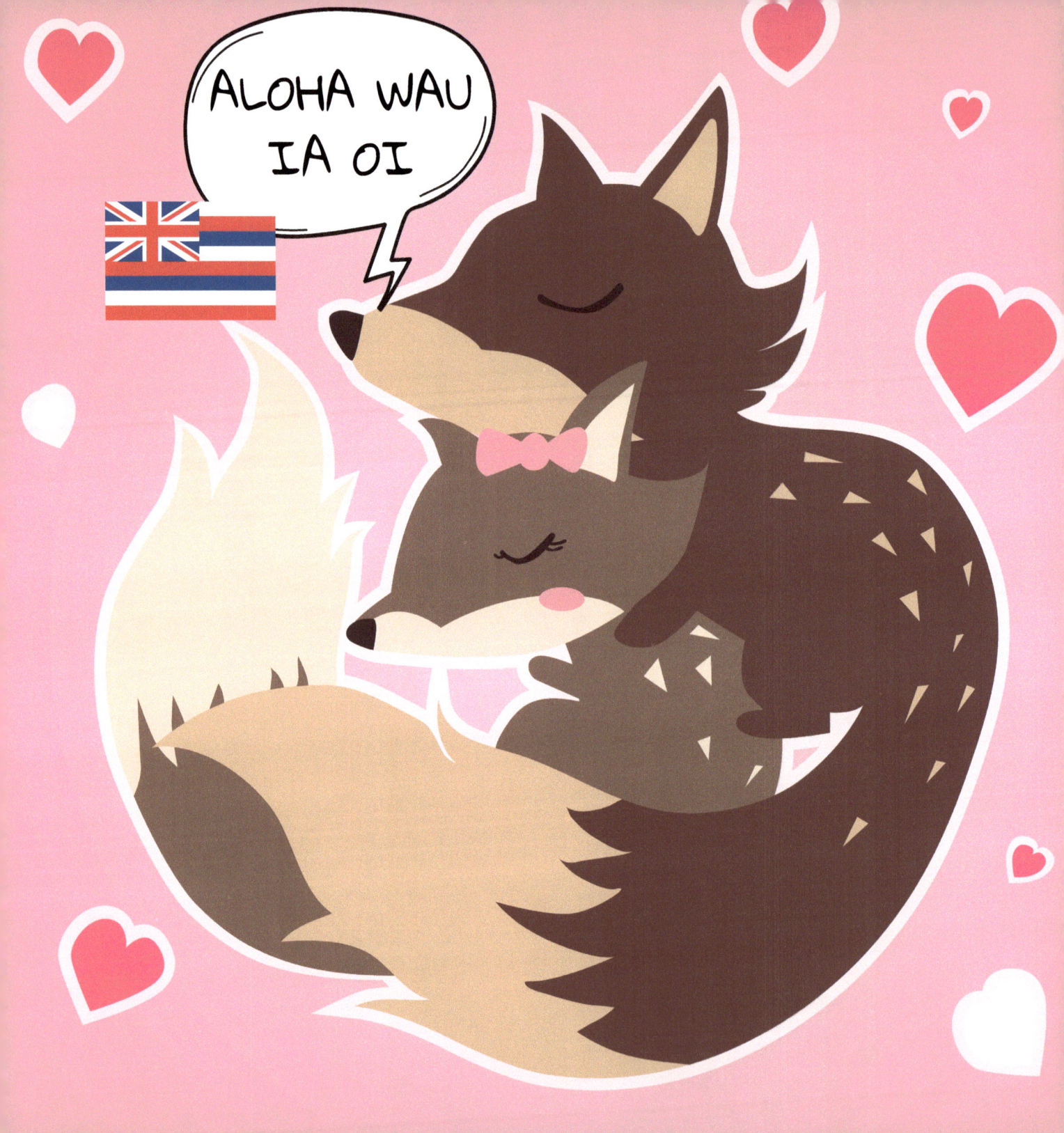

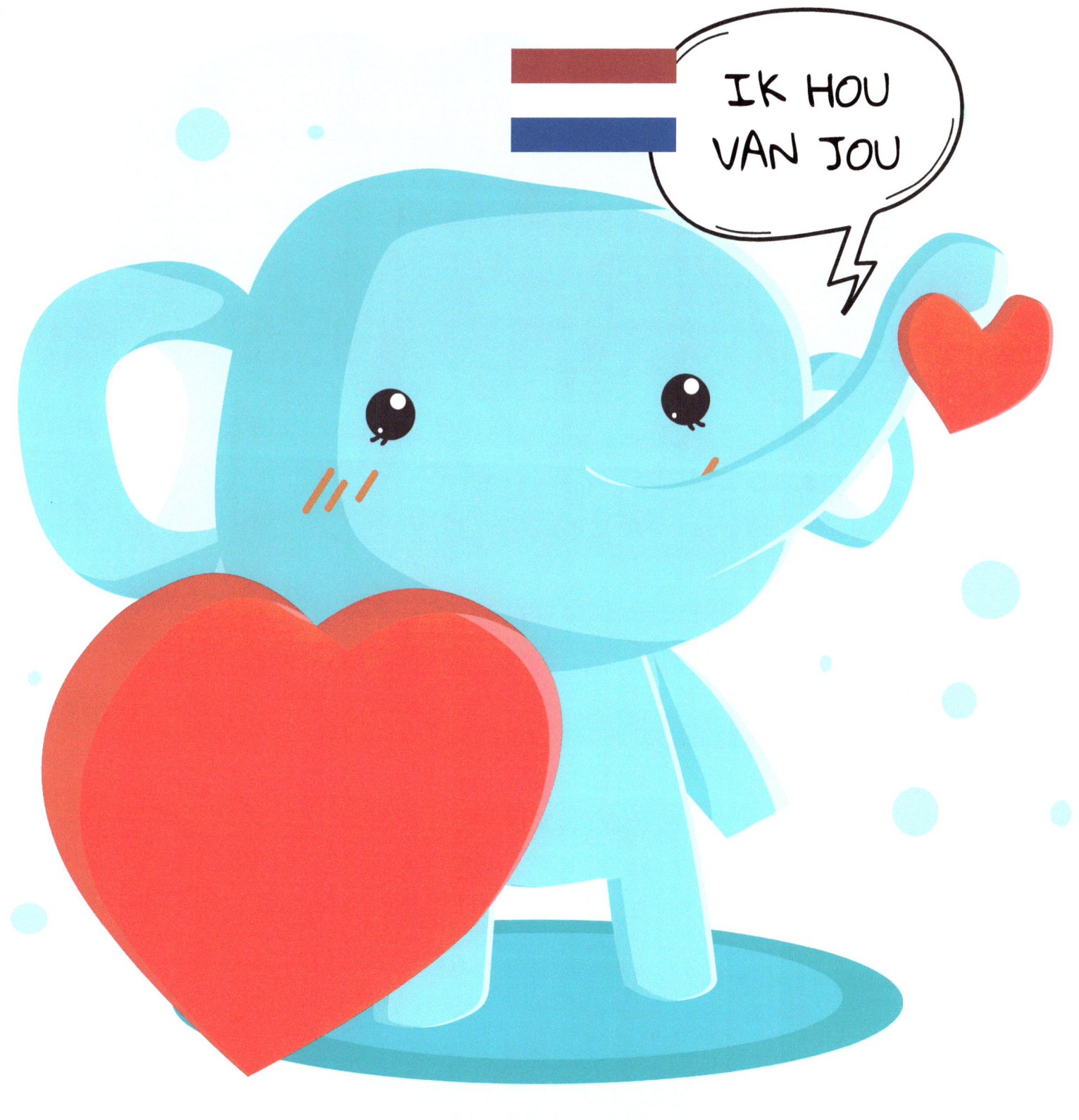

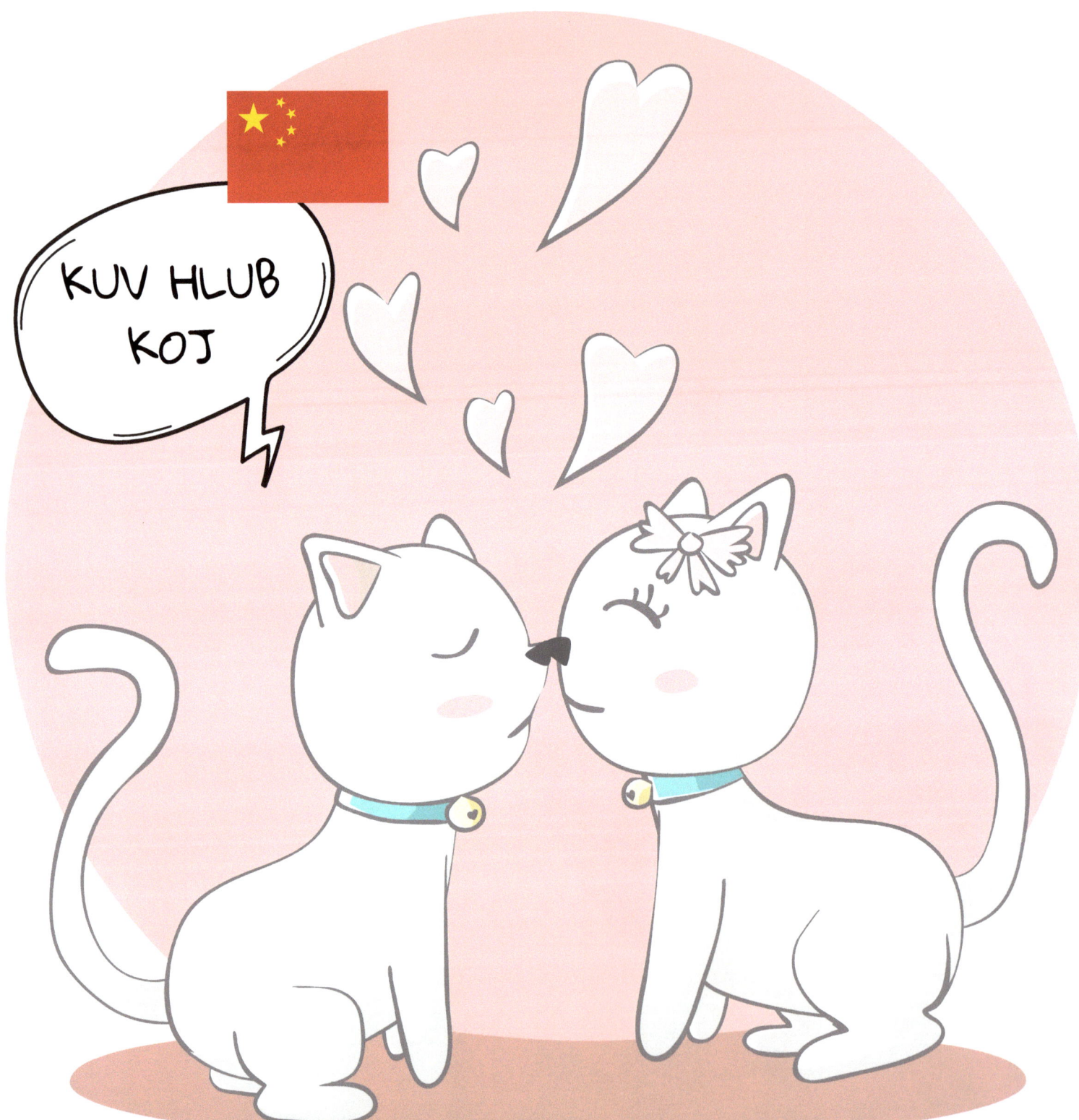

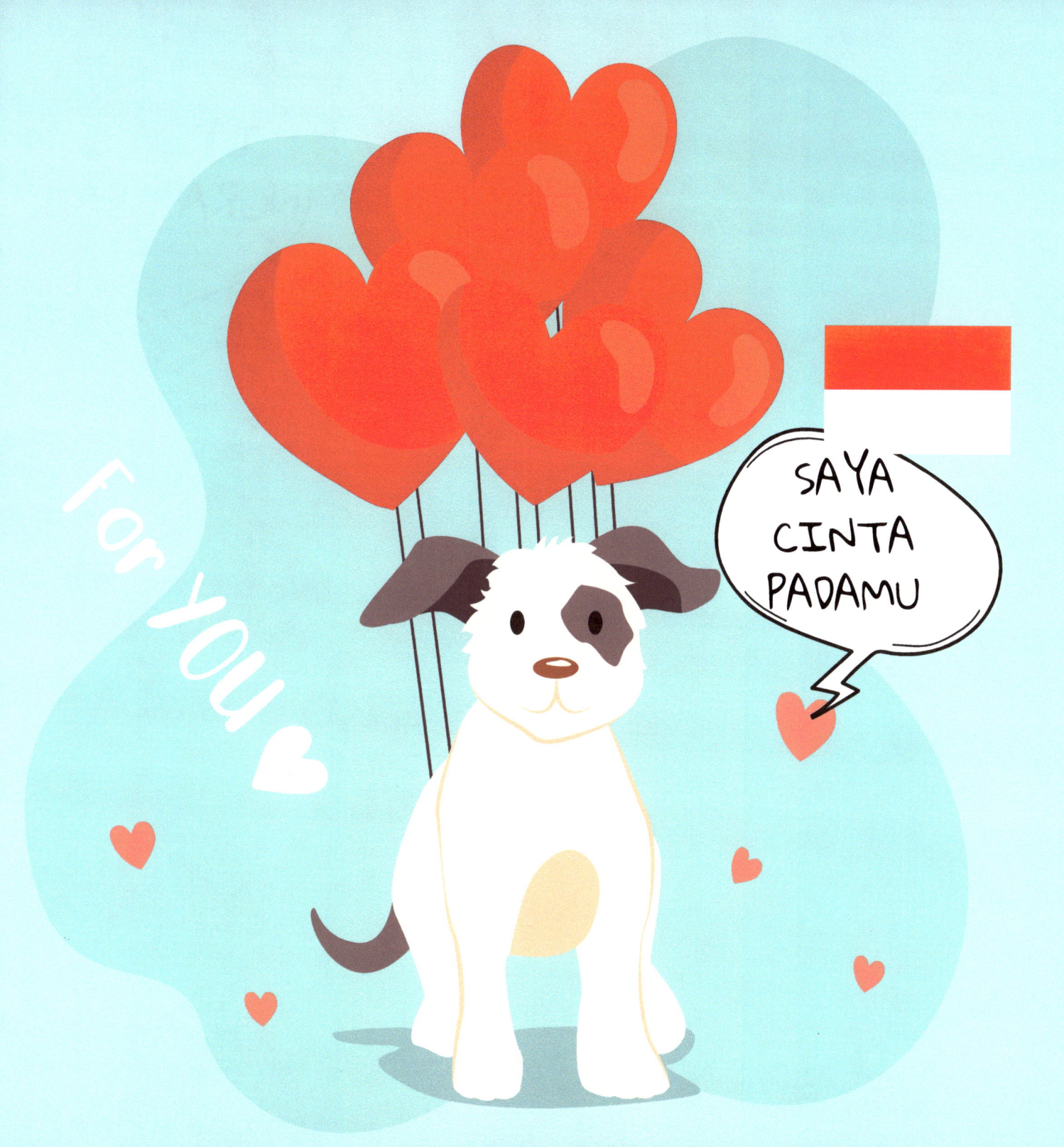

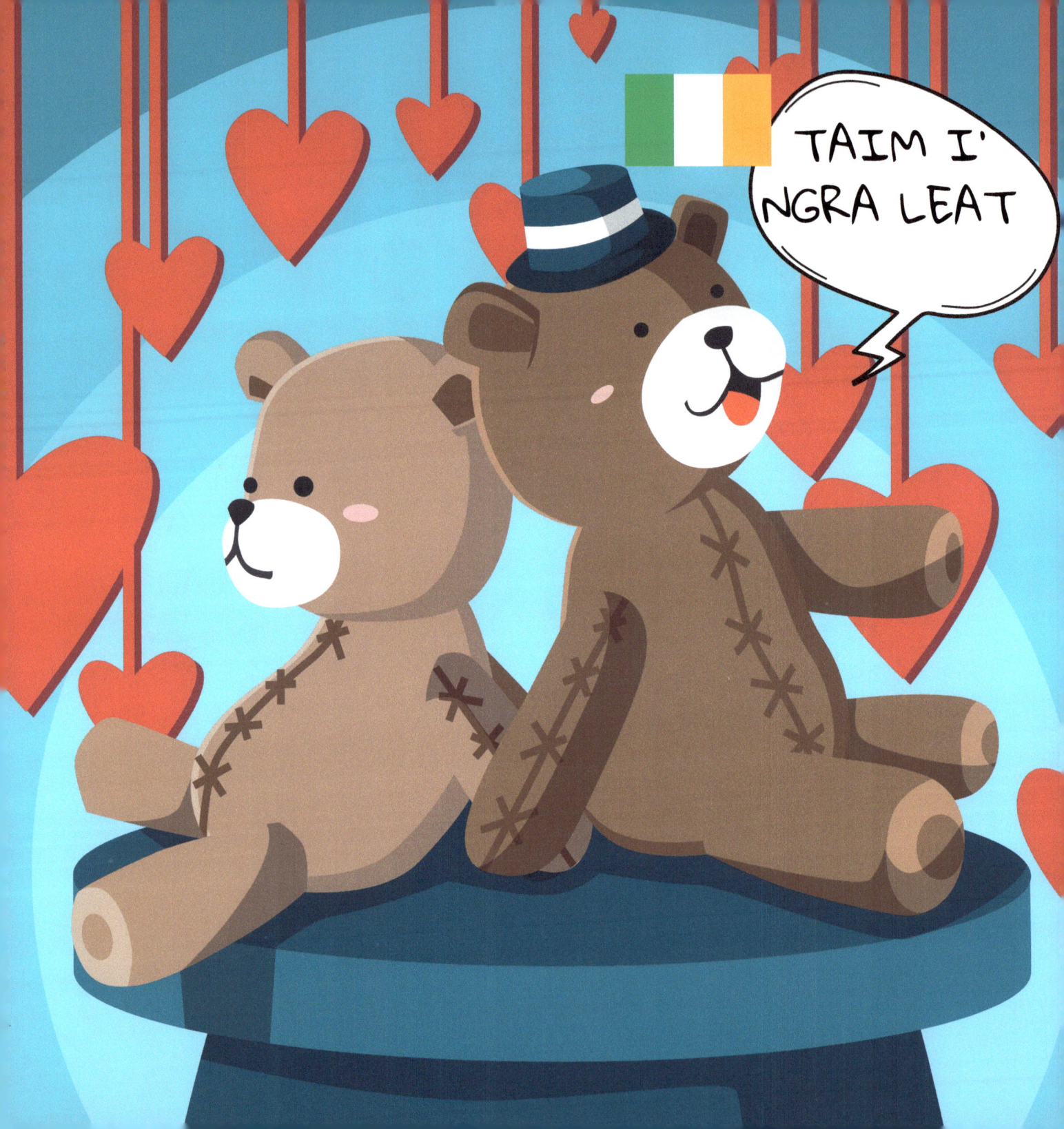

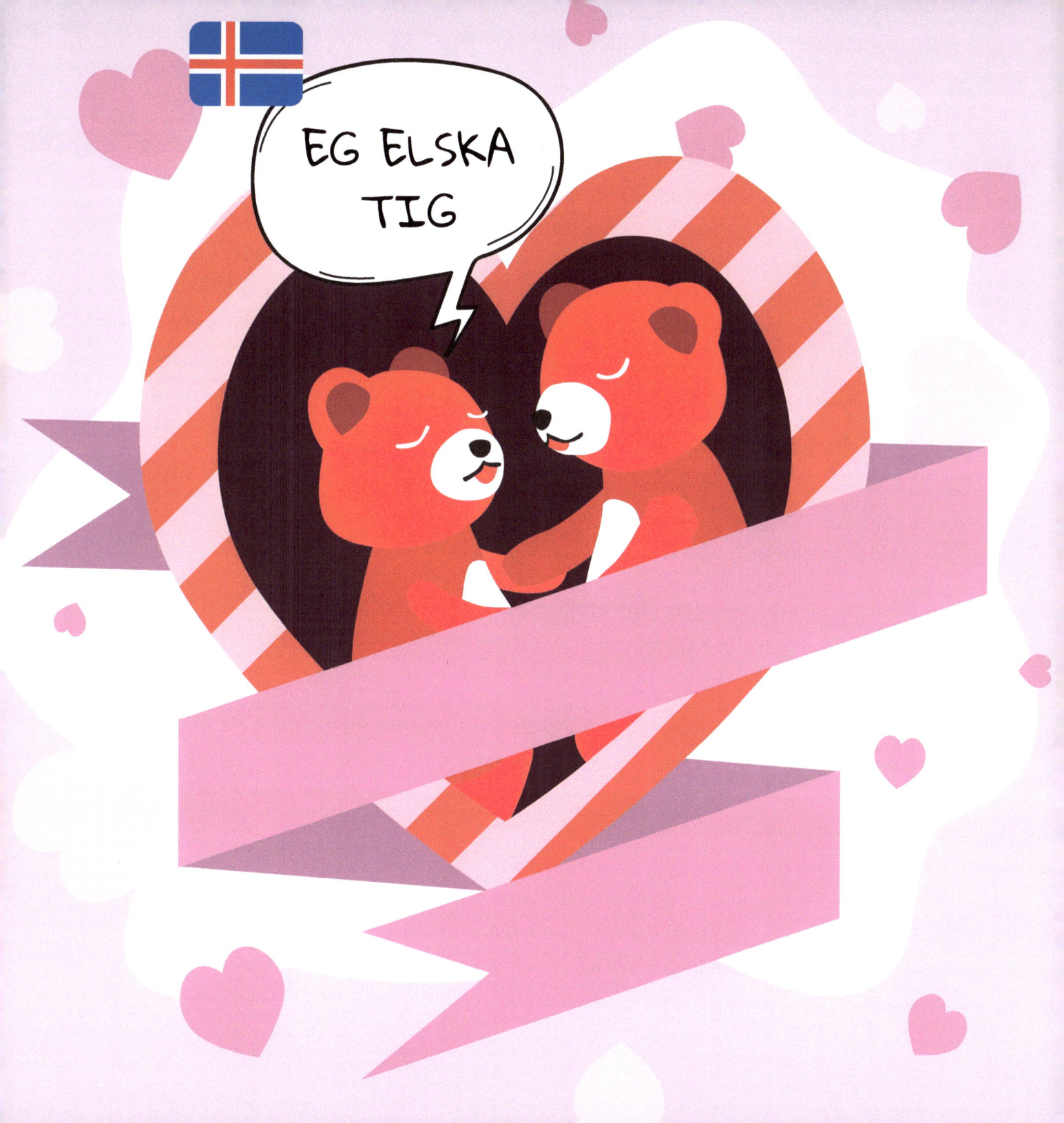

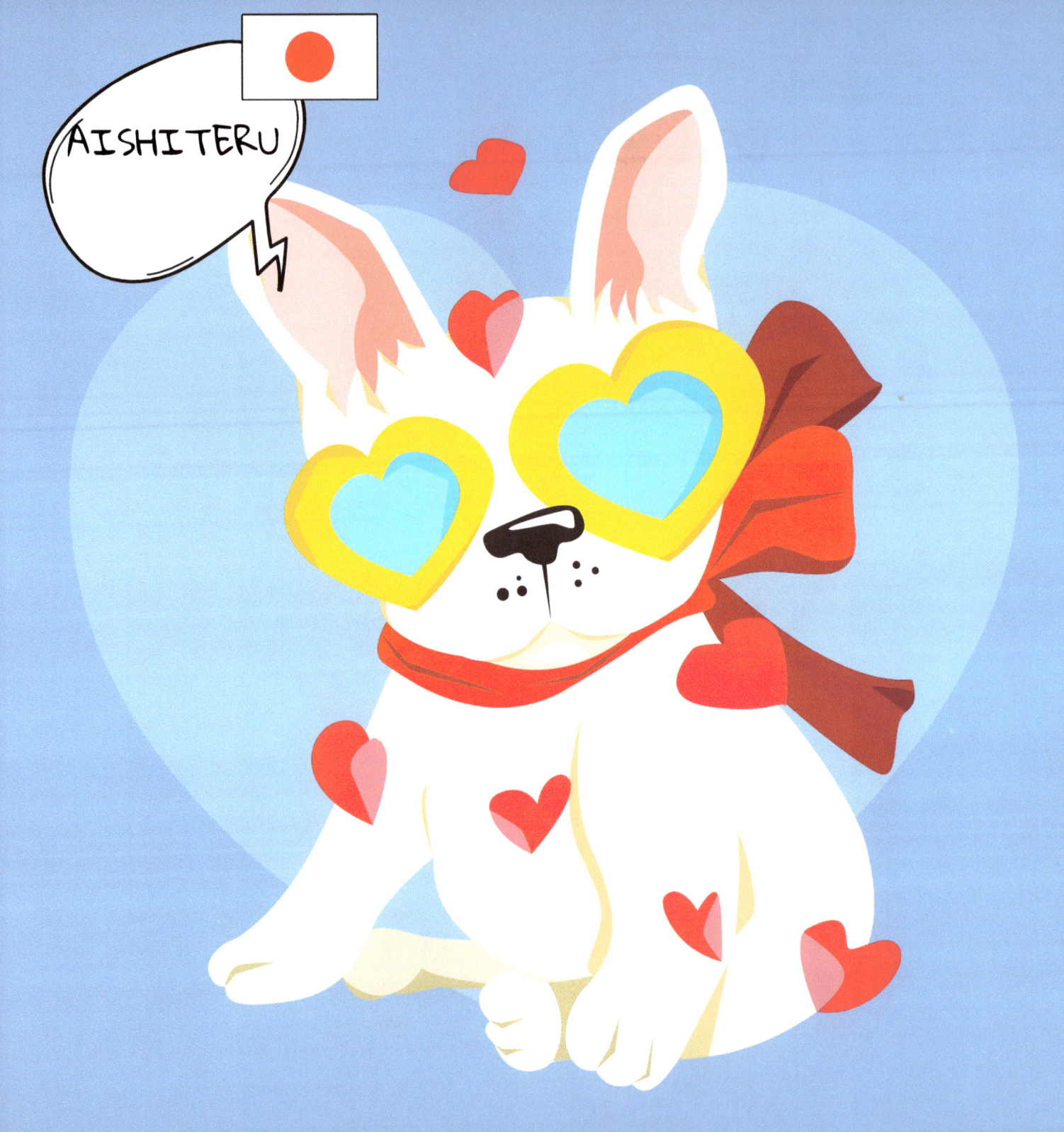

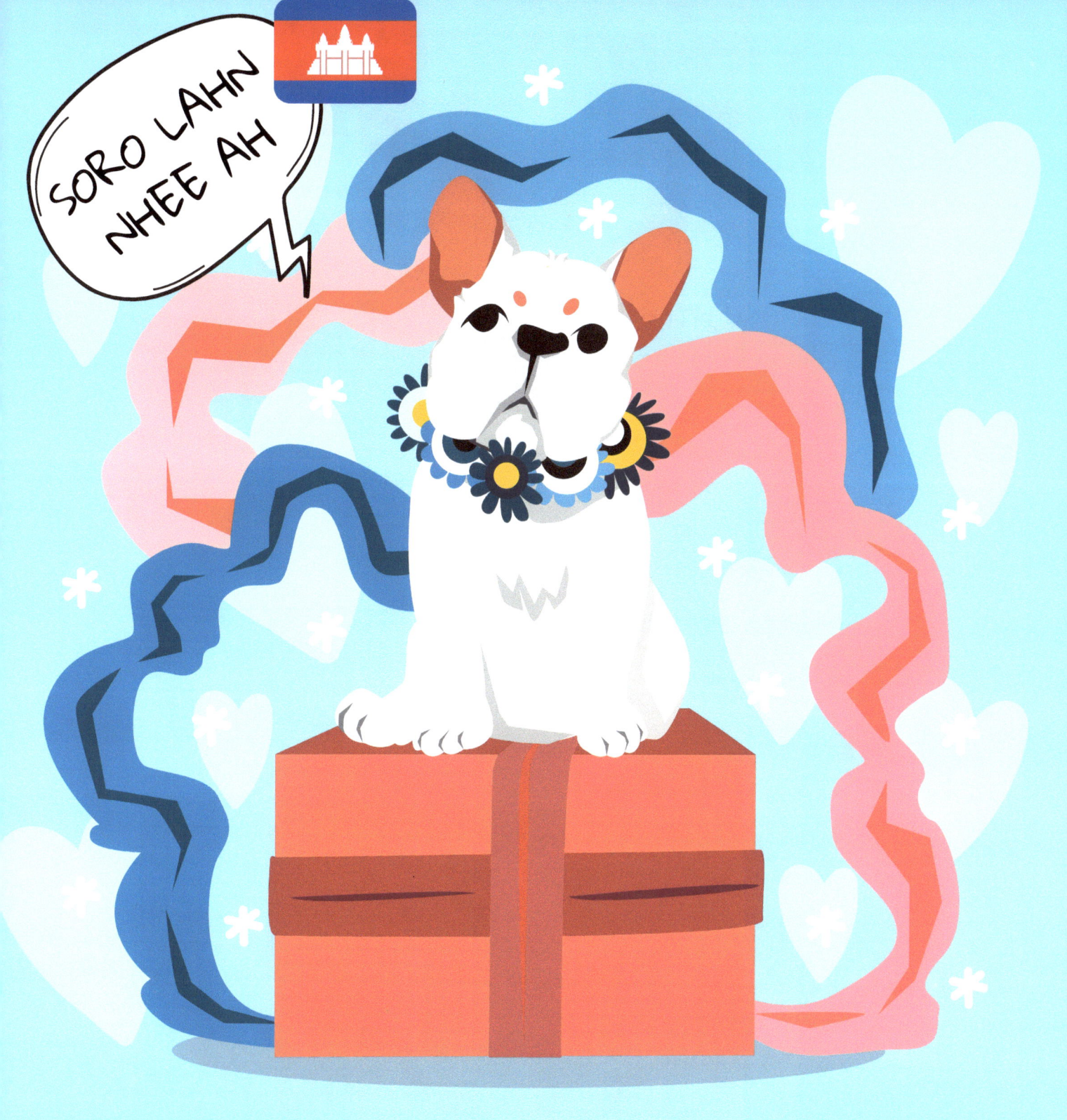

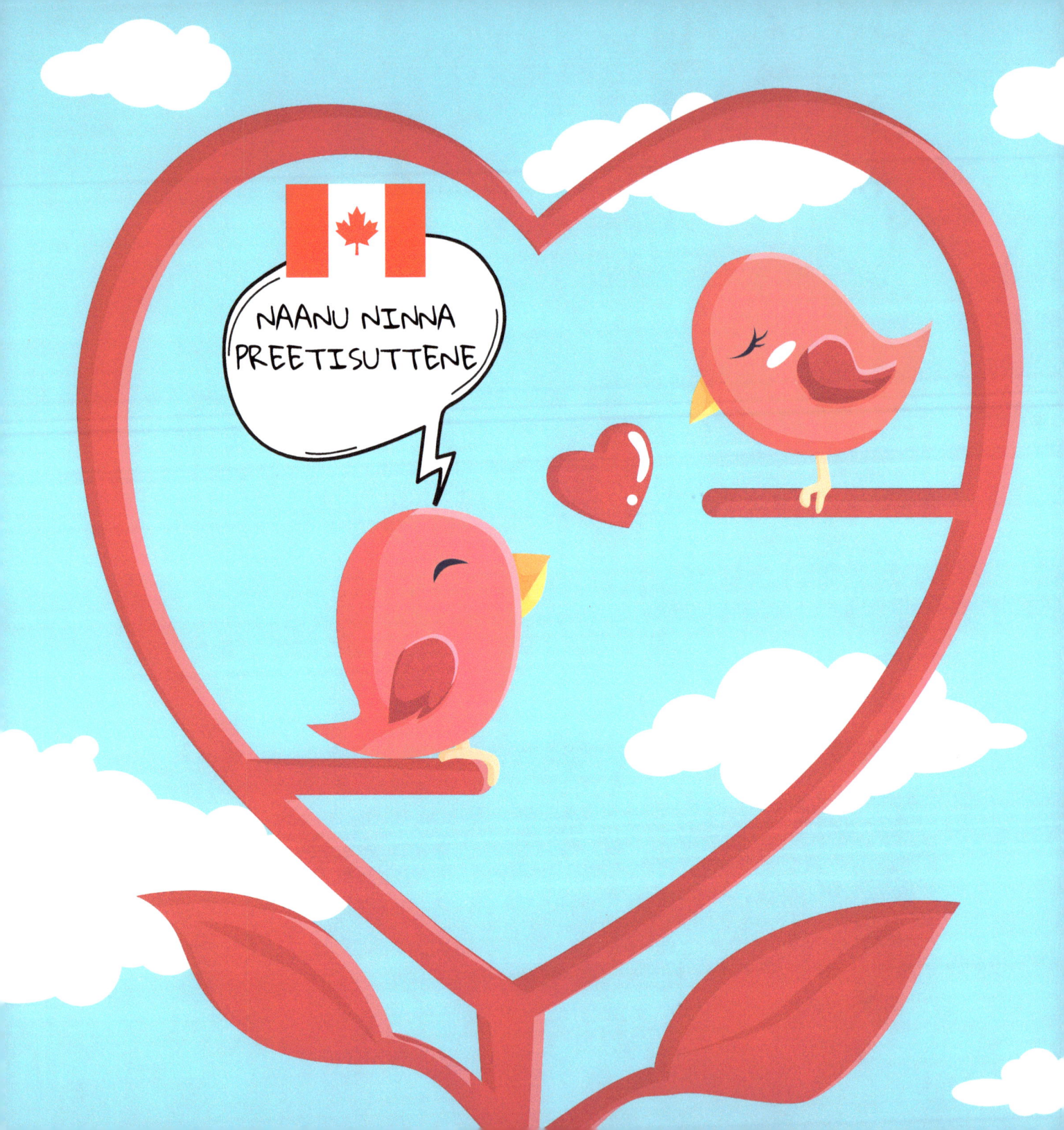

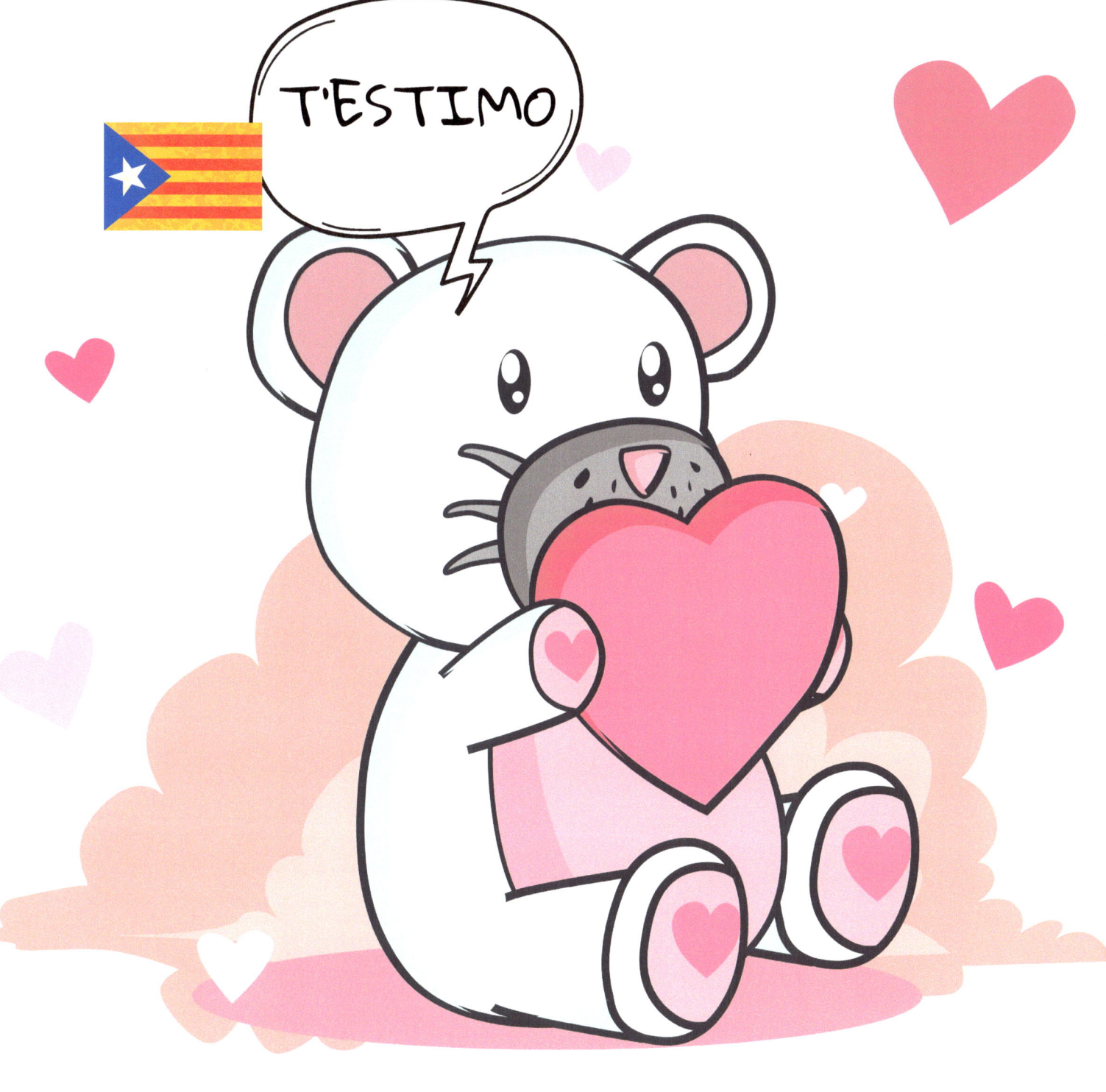

www.ingramcontent.com/pod-product-compliance
Lightning Source LLC
Chambersburg PA
CBHW051821210526
45473CB00005B/1696